THE BUNBURY BOOK
OF LIMERICKS

THE BUNBURY BOOK OF LIMERICKS

being a commonplace collection of
that most particular form of verse
both ancient and modern

by

The Reverend Septimus Bunbury MA

(sometime Chaplain of St Swithun's
College, Cambridge)

Queen Anne Press
Futura

A Queen Anne Press/Futura BOOK

© The Reverend Septimus Bunbury

First published in Great Britain in 1988 by
Queen Anne Press, a division of
Macdonald & Co (Publishers) Ltd
3rd Floor
Greater London House
Hampstead Road
London NW1 7QX

A Pergamon Press plc Company
This edition published in 1988 by
Queen Anne Press/Futura
Illustrations by
McLachlan

ISBN 0 7088 3757 3

Reproduced, printed and bound in Great Britain by
Hazell, Watson & Viney Ltd
Aylesbury, Bucks

CONTENTS

INTRODUCTION

THE GENESIS OF THIS SMALL VOLUME IS FIRMLY ROOTED in the realms of the purely unintentional. Thus, if my good readers will bear with me, I would be unfeignedly thankful for the opportunity to expand further upon the contingent circumstances.

During my chaplaincy at St Swithun's, I bore of course an incumbent responsibility for each and every member of the college. I chose to address myself to this not inconsiderable duty by means of a regular series of invitations, whereby groups of new undergraduates would attend in my rooms, either for tea or, on occasions, dessert; my poor emoluments effectively confining my hospitality within the strictest limits.

I well recall that, having opened our proceedings with a short prayer followed by a few words of welcome to St Swithun's — not I must own one of the best endowed foundations within the University — I would announce a particular passage from the scriptures, thereafter bravely encouraging some degree of free discourse to develop; my intention being the identification of my new charges on an individual basis.

I trust that it will not be construed as a comment upon me, but rather upon a healthy measure of untrammelled student exuberance, that these little verses and the quotations with which they are hopefully leavened, constitute in retrospect the major legacy of our congregations. Suffice it to state that, almost in the twinkling of an eye, my duteous gatherings had become so pandemic in their popularity that, shortly before each appointed hour, phalanxes of be-gowned bicyclists were to be observed emerging from the medieval gateways of colleges great and small, like starlings eager for the roost, their courses set with perilous phreneticism toward my rooms in St Swithun's! Swithun's!

It is only now, in the late afternoon of my years, that I have at last allowed myself to be persuaded to submit my carefully annotated recollections of those happy times for scrutiny by a wider public. And having embarked upon the process of submission with an altogether unconfident heart, imagine if you will my surprise at receiving, through the ever efficient offices of my agent, a response from a most august figure in the publishing world — himself by happy coincidence a Cambridge man — expressing more than a passing interest, albeit with his reservations neatly encapsulated thus:

Now please do not think me a prude,
But your limericks are rather rude.
    So could you revise
      Or — I'd venture — excise
The ones that are specially lewd?

I have to confess that I experienced substantial and recurrent waves both of shock and shame at the initial reaction of this literary panjandrum as, hitherto, I had observed nothing in my manuscript of a less than wholesome or moral nature. However, at this juncture, it could be cardinal for me to admit that my upbringing was, for the most part, entrusted to a sainted spinster aunt, resident in the Cotswold village of Bourton-on-the-Water; my parents having been otherwise occupied in their valiant missionary work, from which neither of them were ever to return, deep within the Middle Congo. Furthermore, it should be noted that I read classics and theology and thus had neither time nor inclination to do other than distance myself from any study of Anglo-Saxon.

Thus it was something of a rude awakening for me, at a most advanced age, to nibble, if not to eat, of the fruit of the tree of life, and to learn, among other things, of that which the Greeks call *euphemism* and also of that to which the French refer as *double entendre*. However, mercifully there is much that I intend will for ever remain to me a mystery. After all, my part in this, akin to that of the Moabite widow Ruth, has merely been that of a gleaner. Consequently, and should further exculpation be expedient, I am honour bound to abrogate authorship, freely according that credit to the merry multitude of seekers after truth which swept through my life, partaking liberally as it went of my caddy (best Typhoo) and decanter (Emva Cream no less).

In concusion dear reader, before you rush headlong into that which follows, pause awhile and permit me to caution you with this small caveat. Mark it well!

> If these limericks need some excusing
> Their wit is not all unamusing.
>> 'Twixt the good and the bad
>> I advise you my lad
> To employ some discretion in choosing.

Septimus Bunbury
Clerk in Holy Orders.

THE CLEVER MEN
AT OXFORD

The clever men at Oxford
Know all that there is to be knowed.
But they none of them know one half as much
As intelligent Mr Toad.

> *The Wind in the Willows*
> Kenneth Grahame 1859-1932

A student at Pembroke named Breeze,
Weighed down with BAs and Litt. Ds,
    Collapsed from the strain:
    And alas, it was plain,
He was killing himself — by degrees.

A Classical Master of Arts
Confessed to his wife he liked tarts.
    Said she 'Well that's fine
    But don't step out of line.
Just remember your principal parts.'

A student of Hertford named Hunt
Was punting his girl in a punt
    When she said, 'On the whole,
    While you're wielding that pole,
I'd prefer you avoided my front.'

Whenever he goes to the privvy,
A student from Brasenose named Shrivvy
    Exercises his mind
    Then wipes his behind
With some well-chosen pages of Livy.

Oxford was like a chat show, but with more people.
Alan Coren

At Christ Church, the dirty old Dean
Said 'The funniest jokes are obscene.
    For to bowdlerise wit
    Takes the pith out of it.
And who wants a funny that's clean?'

A choirboy from Magdalen named Bean
Has a sex-life that's somewhat unclean.
    He receives Divine Unction
    Through anal conjunction
And can't get enough: he's that keen.

To the University of Oxford I acknowledge no
obligation; and she will as cheerfully renounce me for
a son, as I am willing to disclaim her for a mother.
I spent fourteen months at Magdalen College: they
proved the fourteen months the most idle and
unprofitable of my whole life.

                           Autobiography
                    Edward Gibbon 1737-94

A New College freshman named Spears
Once spent a weekend with two queers.
    And although we've enquired
    He won't say what transpired —
But he hasn't sat down for two years!

There was a young student from Oriel
Who flouted the ruling proctorial
    When he ran down the Corn
    With one hell of a horn
And buggered the Martyrs' Memorial.

In Oxford a Fellow of Worcester
Had a keen, red-hot, Rhode Island Rooster.
    But as he got older
    His rooster grew colder,
And could no longer peck like it used ter.

A young Merton man, somewhat queer,
Tried to bugger the Dean in the rear.
    Said the old man 'Fun's fun,
    But I really must run.
So be quick now and come, there's a dear.'

Very nice sort of place, Oxford, I should think, for
people that like that sort of place.
                    Man and Superman, Act II
                    George Bernard Shaw 1856-1950

A Somerville student named Marge,
Plunged nude in the Thames from a barge.
    Then a don, from a punt,
    Introduced up her cunt
An organ amazingly large.

A sculler from Univ. named Box
Forced the Oxford eight onto the rocks.
     The crew shouted 'Bollocks!
     You've ripped off our rowlocks
And grievously injured our cox.'

TO CAMBRIDGE – BOOKS

The King, observing with judicious eyes
The state of both his universities,
To Oxford sent a troop of horse, and why?
That learned body wanted loyalty;
To Cambridge books, as very well discerning
How much that loyal body wanted learning.
> On George I's donation of the Bishop of Ely's
> library to Cambridge University
> Joseph Trapp 16979-1747

A Peterhouse man, sweet and tender,
Went out with two dons on a bender.
    And after three days
    He returned in a haze,
No longer quite sure of his gender.

Said a naughty young nancy from Trinity:
'I'm delighted I've lost my virginity.
    I've a thing about men
    And I admit — now and then —
I enjoy them about my vicinity.'

A frustrated young student from Clare
Knelt down in the moonlight, all bare,
    And prayed to his God
    For a romp on the sod.
'Twas a Corpus man answered the prayer.

From Fitzwilliam, a student named Fender
Said 'Sir, I declare I surrender.
    I've had more than enough
    And the going's got tough:
And I fear you are of the wrong gender!'

Atque inter silvas Academi quaerere verum.
And seek for truth in the groves of Academe.
Epistles II.ii.45
Horace 65-8 BC

The virtuous ladies of Newnham
Are preserved from the men who would ruin 'em
    By the tales that they've heard
    Of young gels who have erred,
And the morals their teachers imbue in 'em.

A frustrated young freshman from John's
Attempted to bugger the swans.
>   But he was caught by the porter
>   Who said 'Sir, try my daughter,
For the swans are reserved for the dons.'

The desire of a Caius man named Eric
Is to be 'had' in a manner Homeric:
>   Which implies 'twixt the cheeks,
>   In the way of the Greeks,
Since he deems other methods barbaric.

From women's eyes this doctrine I derive:
They are the ground, the books, the academes,
From whence doth spring the true Promethean fire.
>   *Love's Labour's Lost*
>   William Shakespeare 1564-1616

There was a young student, Maud Burton
Who outraged the Mistress of Girton
>   By cycling to town
>   Without wearing a gown;
And what's worse, without even a skirt on.

Said the Dean on the banks of the Cam:
'See the girl in that punt? What a lamb!
      With one bound and a leap
      I should shepherd that sheep
But I've an urge to behave like a ram.'

At Downing a student named Dick
Was endowded with a marvellous prick.
      From its tip, like a prism,
      He could shoot enough gism
To make any cocksucker sick.

England is still governed from ... Shrewsbury School,
from Cambridge, with their annexes of the Stock
Exchange and the solicitors' offices ...
                    George Bernard Shaw 1856-1950

There was a young freshman from Queens'
Who frequented the market latrines
      Until caught in a lock-up
      In the act, with his cock up
Two fellows called Milton and Keynes.

A scholar of King's named Maclean
Regrettably upset the Dean
    By flooding the college
    With intimate knowledge
Of subjects perverse and obscene.

A fellow of Corpus named Wipple
Loved to tweak-up a Girton girl's nipple:
    As her titties grew harder
    He'd stir up her ardour
So she'd climax with hardly a ripple.

A student from Emma, named Rafferty
Went down to the gentlemen's lavatory. (pron.
lafferti)
    When the walls met his sight
    He said 'Newton *was* right.
This *must* be the centre of graffiti.'

A LITTLE LEARNING

A little learning is a dang'rous thing;
An Essay on Criticism
Alexander Pope 1688-1744

Said a student from York University,
When asked about sexual diversity,
'Copulation's OK,
In the old-fashioned way,
But I do like a touch of perversity.'

A learned professor from Buckingham
Wrote a thesis on cocks and on sucking 'em;
But the next year his work
Was eclipsed by a Turk,
With a treatise on fannies and fucking 'em.

A professor of Latin at London
Feared females so much that he shunned 'em.
    While his sex drive urged 'Go',
    He exclaimed 'no, no, no.
Illegitimi non carborundum.'

There was a young man from Cornell
Who complained, 'I'm aware of a smell.
    But whether it's drains
    Or human remains,
I'm really unable to tell.'

Sociology Degrees — Help yourself.
                 Graffiti: above lavatory-paper holder
                      at one of the newer universities

A middle-aged strumpet from Yale
Had her price list tattooed on her tail.
    And her plump pink behind,
    For the sake of the blind
Read 'Reductions for Parties', in braille!

A palaeontologist — Locke —
Found a fossilised Jurassic cock.
   'It's Tyrannosaurus:
    Long, thick, black and porous.
And wow! It's still hard as a rock!'

❧

In a post-alcoholic euphoria,
A classical don, near Victoria
   Was discovered one day
   In a club for the gay,
Immersed in an *Ars Amatoria*.

They are the books, the arts, the academes,
That show, contain, and nourish all the world.
              Love's Labour's Lost
        William Shakespeare 1564-1616

Far dearer to me than my treasure'
Miss Guggenheim said 'Is my leisure.
   For I do love to screw
   The entire Harvard crew.
They're slow, but it lengthens the pleasure.'

Our Old Nobility

Let wealth and commerce, laws and learning die,
But leave us still our old nobility!

England's Trust
Lord John Manners, Duke of Rutland 1818-1906

Did you know that the Duchess of Belvoir
Goes to bed with her Golden Retriever?
  Says the disgusted Duke
  'Such a thing makes me puke.
Were it not for her money, I'd leave her!'

At the table sat young Lord Colquhoun,
With his pet, an old red-bummed baboon.
  His mother said 'Cholmondley,
  I don't think it comely
To encourage that creature to moon.'

20

The bashful Viscountess of Dee
Sings loudly when having a pee.
　　It's so that during the latter
　　She can drown out the splatter,
And not as a mere *jeu d'esprit*.

At death's door lay old Lady Phipps.
No man had yet mounted her hips.
　　So the postillion tried her;
　　By Heck, did he ride her!
And she died with a smile on her lips.

The frigid old Viscountess Gloucester
Hired a gigolo named Freddy Foster.
　　She was poked by this pro
　　Seven weeks in a row —
It took the first six to defrost her.

Now really young man, you're a bore',
Said the Lady Lavinia Wills-Gore.
 'I'm all covered in sweat,
 And you haven't come yet;
And Good Lord; it's a quarter past four!'

I'm as drunk as the lord that I am!
   John Betjeman 1906-1984,
quoting inebriated undergraduate peer in 1933.

There was a Countess from The Chase
Who was woefully lacking in grace.
 In the midst of a kiss
 She started to piss:
Which was neither the time nor the place.

The Dowager Duchess of Chester
Fell madly in love with a jester.
 Though she reacted most hotly
 At the sight of his motley,
'Twas the tip of his wand most impressed her.

For his birthday, a Duke of Great Britain
Was given a bath-chair to sit in;
    A rug for his floor
    And a brass cuspidor
And a new coronet, just to spit in.

A fully equipped duke costs as much to keep up as two
dreadnoughts; and dukes are just as great a terror and
they last longer.

               David Lloyd George 1863-1945

That prudish old Lady Montcrieff
Has riches beyond all belief.
    But she spends most of her boodle
    On a pampered pink poodle
Whose 'rude bits' she hides 'neath a leaf.

The manners of Lady Cathcart
I find more offensive than smart.
    For whenever I come
    She lifts high her vast bum
And lets off an earth-shaking fart.

The dirty old Duchess of Wick
Said 'I'm tired of sucking your prick.
    It's not that I funk
    At the taste of your spunk:
But the smell of your balls makes me sick!'

Said the passionate Countess of Ewell,
'All the boys want of course is my jewel.
    But I make my selection
    By length of erection.
Ten inches is fine — as a rule.'

It was but a few weeks since he had taken his seat in
the Lords; and this afternoon, for the want of anything
better to do, he strayed in and sat in it.

Zuleika Dobson
Sir Max Beerbohm 1872-1956

Sir Reginald Beaumondsey, Bart.,
For a masked ball had dressed as a fart
    By painting his face
    Like a most private place;
His cough made the Dowagers start.

A young chorus girl, Gorgeous Gloria
Was 'had' by Sir Gerald du Maurier,
　　Jack Hilton, Jack Payne,
　　Then Sir Gerald — again,
And the band at the Waldorf Astoria.

A determined young footman named Lyle
Said 'I'll roger Her Grace of Argyll!'
　　But on the job — what a joke —
　　He died of a stroke;
So the Duke had him buried in style.

To his bride quoth Sir Wulstan Fitz-Dawes,
'Lock this chastity belt round your drawers!'
　　But a determined old Celt
　　Picked the lock of the belt
While the knight was away at the wars.

THE QUALITY OF MERCY

The quality of mercy is not strain'd;
The Merchant of Venice
William Shakespeare 1564-1616

At Gray's Inn, a student of law
Declared 'Legal wording's a bore.
    Is there anything dafter
      Than to say "hereinafter"
And "whereas" and "heretobefore"?'

A young lady lawyer named Hawte
Was undoubtedly guilty of tort.
    For she'd pee in the tea
      Of the leading QC,
Then strip-off in the well of the court.

It is illegal to make liquor privately or water publicly.
Lord Birkett b. 1929

In the Temple a lawyer named Rex
Was sadly deficient in sex.
        When charged with exposure
        He replied, with composure:
'*De minimis non curat lex*!'

(The Law does not care about such small matters)

A certain schoolmarm from Devizes
Was had up at the local Assizes
        For teaching young boys
        Matrimonial joys,
And giving french letters as prizes.

Laws were made to be broken.
Noctes Ambrosianae
Christopher North 1785-1854

A beefy young copper named Plod,
Renowned for the size of his rod,
    Attempted to stuff it
    Up little Miss Muffet.
The last words she spoke were 'My God!'

A corpulent fellow named Hyatt
Liked to gobble young men on the quiet.
    But he was caught on a wharf
    Going down on a dwarf.
So he pleaded he'd gone on a diet.

An inmate of Parkhurst named Sissons
Was upset by his nightly emissions.
    His cell mate, a queer,
    Said 'Don't fret yourself dear.'
And taught him all fifty positions.

A maiden from far Samarkand
In the nude tried to dance down the Strand.
    But in the Queen's Bench Division
    She was informed — with derision
'Such exotic cavortings are banned.'

A mortician, arrested in Fife,
Had made love to the corpse of his wife.
    'How could I know Judge?
      She was cold — didn't budge —
Just the same as she'd been all her life.'

There was a young lady from Wantage
Of whom the town clerk took advantage.
    Said the borough surveyor
    'I think you should pay her,
'Cos you've altered the line of her frontage.'

Nisi per legale iudicium parium suorom vel per legem terrae.
Except by the legal judgement of his peers or by the law of the land.

Clause 39
Magna Carta, 1215

THE ROYAL BANNERS
FORWARD GO

Vexilla regis prodeunt.
Venantius Fortunatus c. 535-c. 600

Most Gracious Queen, we thee implore
To go away and sin no more,
But if that effort be too great,
To go away at any rate.

Epigram on Queen Caroline, 1820,
quoted in Lord Colchester's diary

Queen Mary found Scotsmen are built
With a decidedly angular tilt.
To her regal surprise
Every member would rise
Every time she groped under a kilt.

Everyone likes flattery; and when you come to Royalty
you should lay it on with a trowel.

Remark to Matthew Arnold
Benjamin Disraeli, Earl of Beaconsfield 1804-81

There once was a monarch called Ed
Who took Mrs Simpson to bed.
    As they bounced up and down
    He said 'Bugger the Crown.
We'll give it to Albert instead!'

A snooty young lady at Court
Enquired of the Prince, with a snort,
    'Was it humour, or shyness
    That prompted your Highness
To doctor my fruit-cup with port?'

Curtsey while you're thinking what to say. It saves time.
Through the Looking-Glass
Lewis Carroll (Charles Lutwidge Dodgson) 1832-98

'Golly gosh!' said Prince Percy of Wales:
'I've just heard what marriage entails.
    So in place of a girl
    I'd like a pretty young Earl.
You see, I've a penchant for males.'

'Where shall I begin, please your Majesty?' he asked.
'Begin at the beginning' the King said, gravely, 'and go
on till you come to the end: then stop.'
                    Alice's Adventures in Wonderland
       Lewis Carroll (Charles Lutwidge Dodgson) 1832-98

Have you heard about Shakespeare's King Lear?
He drank whisky along with his beer.
        And, imbibing this potion,
        Was overcome with emotion
And buggered the barmaid's plump rear!

How You Played
the Game

For when the One Great Scorer comes
To write against your name,
He marks — not that you won or lost —
But how you played the game.
Alumnus Football
Grantland Rice 1880-1954

'The bedwooms are full' said Miranda
To her beau with commendable candour.
        'And the antique chaise longue
        Is not vewy stwrong.
So why don't we twy the vewandah?'

A widow who lived in Bermuda
Once thrashed a marauding intruder.
        It was not just her ire
        At his lack of attire,
But his nicking her jewels as he screwed her!

34

It's worse than wicked, my dear — it's vulgar.
Punch Almanac 1876

A determined young lady of taste
Liked to keep herself virgin and chaste
    And stoutly defended
    With gin traps suspended
On filigree chains, from her waist.

There was a posh lady called Hopper,
Who came a society cropper.
    She went to Ostend
    With a gentleman friend —
The rest of this story's improper.

My name is George Nathaniel Curzon,
I am a most superior person.
My face is pink, my hair is sleek,
I dine at Blenheim once a week.
The Masque of Balliol c. 1877

An elderly lady from Bude
Was such a meticulous prude
    That she pulled down the blind
    When changing her mind,
Lest some passer-by should intrude.

We are, we are, we know we are —
    Superior!

Anonymous

Said an old English gent, quite a toff,
'Now top up your glasses; let's quaff
    To short skirted joys,
    Which enable the boys
To begin where their fathers left off.'

But his Captain's hand on his shoulder smote —
'Play up! play up! and play the game!'

The Island Race
Sir Henry John Newbolt 1862-1938

A Sloane Ranger gel named Priscilla
Used to flavour her 'bits' with vanilla.
    The result was so fine
    Not just men queued in line
But also a silver chinchilla.

A sorry old spinster named Ruth
Often wept when she thought of her youth;
    And the marvellous chances
    She'd missed at school dances
And once in a telephone booth.

MOMENTS MUSICALES

The man that hath no music in himself,
Nor is not mov'd with concord of sweet sounds,
Is fit for treasons, stratagems, and spoils;
The motions of his spirit are dull as night,
And his affections dark as Erebus:
Let no such man be trusted.

The Merchant of Venice
William Shakespeare 1564-1616

A deep baritone from Havana,
While singing slipped on a banana.
    He took ill for a year,
      Then resumed his career
As a *coloratura soprana*!

A young violinist from Rio
Made love to a 'cellist called Cleo.
    As he ripped off her panties
    He said 'Forget your *andantes*.
I prefer it *allegro con brio*.'

❧

A musical King called Canute
Was alarmed by the warts on his root.
    He put acid on these
    And now, when he pees,
He can tootle his tool like a flute.

> Sing a song of sixpence,
> A pocketful of rye.
> *Tommy Thumb's Pretty Song Book* (c 1744)

Two piano duetists from Cheam
Would even make love as a team.
    One aft and one frontal,
    With strokes contrapuntal
They developed a fucking good theme.

> Please do not shoot the pianist. He is doing his best.
> *Impressions of America: Leadville*
> Oscar Wilde 1854-1900

A randy *tenore robusto*
Pursues the sopranos *con gusto.*
   In the last act of 'Faust' —
   Yes, I admit he was soused —
He joggled the diva's *bel busto!*

A maestro conducting in Rome
Had an odd way of driving it home.
   The girls that he met
   Had to keep their stroke set
To the beat of his brass metronome.

     Usus promptos facit.
     Practice makes perfect.

The composer, Georg Freidrich Handel,
Whose sexual life was a scandal,
   Grew red in the face
   When he wrote figured bass,
So he buggered himself with a candle.

A sexy young dancer named Sally
Was performing one night in the ballet.
    To tumultuous applause
    She tore off her drawers
And showed off the depth of her valley.

'Music!' she said dreamily; and such is the force of
habit that 'I don't', she added, 'know anything about
music, really. But I know what I like.'
Zuleika Dobson.
Sir Max Beerbohm 1872-1956

At the first night of Carmen, the bass,
To his dying despair and disgrace,
    Did a fart of such violence
    In a moment of siolence
It brought a deep blush to his face.

Sir Thomas, his face like a hatchet,
Observed to a 'cellist from Datchet,
    'You have 'twixt your thighs
    My dear, a great prize;
An instrument noted for beauty and size,
And yet you just sit there and scratch it!!'

FOR BETTER, FOR WORSE

Marriage is popular because it combines the maximum
of temptation with the maximum of opportunity.
Maxims for Revolutionists
George Bernard Shaw 1856-1950

A delighted incredulous bride
Remarked to the groom at her side:
I never could quite
Believe till tonight
Our anatomies *would* coincide.

How To Be Happy Though Married.
Title of Book
E.J. Hardy 1849-1920

A man with venereal fear
Has intercourse in his wife's ear!
She says 'I don't mind,
Except that I find
When the telephone rings, I don't hear.'

43

Upstairs there's a couple from Ealing.
They're on honeymoon, I've a strong feeling.
   They scream while they're grinding
   And, of late, I am finding
A network of cracks on my ceiling!

*

Their bedsprings, what's more, twang and creak
And have kept me awake this past week.
   Oh why do newly-weds
   Use such squeaky beds
To practice their screwing techniques?

❧

On the day of her wedding in Chester
Said her mum to the bride, as she dressed her:
   'My girl, you're in luck.
   'He's a jolly fine fuck,
For I've had him myself once in Leicester.'

> For he's going to marry Yum-Yum —
> Yum-Yum!
>
> *The Mikado*
> Sir William Schwenk Gilbert 1836-1911

An old married couple named Kelly
Have had to live belly to belly;
    Because once, in their haste,
    They used library paste
Instead of petroleum jelly.

Marriage is like life in this — that it is a field of battle,
and not a bed of roses.

                      Virginibus Puerisque
               Robert Louis Stevenson 1850-94

There was a young fellow from Crick
With a willie remarkably thick.
    But he chose a young bride
    With a front door so wide
That they easily managed the trick.

I felt sorry for poor Angus Keating
For his pride took a terrible beating.
    This happens to males
    When they learn the details
Of their wives' extra-marital cheating.

Advice to persons about to marry.
'Don't.'
                    Punch, vol viii, p 1, 1845

There was an old fellow of Fosham
Who took out his bollocks to wash 'em.
        Said his wife 'Listen Jack.
        If you don't put them back
I'll stamp on your scrotum and squash 'em!'

Every woman should marry — and no man.
                    Lothair
Benjamin Disraeli, Earl of Beaconsfield 1804-81

There was an old tailor of Gloucester
Whose wife ran away with a coster.
        He traced her to Leicester
        And tried to arrest her,
But in spite of his efforts — he lost her.

THE CHURCH'S ONE FOUNDATION

Je voudrais, et ce sera le dernier et le plus ardent de mes souhaits, je voudrais que le dernier des rois fût entranglé avec les boyaux du dernier prêtre.
I should like to see, and this will be the last and the most ardent of my desires, I should like to see the last king strangled with the guts of the last priest.

In his Will
Jean Messelier 1664?-1733

There is a young curate of Twickenham
Whose pants have a wonderful prick in 'em.
    But it's more than a shock
    To young girls, when this cock
He whips out and insists he must stick in 'em.

The dark deeds of the Dean of Westminster
Concerned an insatiable spinster.
    To ensure she was clean —
    In spirit, I mean —
He filled up the font first — then rinsed her.

When selecting the Dean of Hong Kong,
They judge by the length of his prong.
    The most firm and erect
    They're sure to elect.
Then 'God Save the Dean' is the song!

Have you heard about Sister Sophia?
She's succumbed to the Abbot's desire,
    Saying 'I know it's a sin,
    But now that you're in —
Please shove it up, higher and higher.'

The incumbent Vicar of Bray
Kept his wife in the family way;
    'Til she became more alert
    And bought a vaginal squirt,
And declared to her spouse, 'Let us spray!'

There was a young choirboy from Crewe
Who declared, as the curate withdrew,
    'Well! The dear vicar was slicker
    And thicker and quicker
And four inches longer than you!'

*

Replied the curate, 'Yes Hugh, you are right:
The vicar's a man of great might.
    But his style's out of fashion —
    And he hasn't my passion,
So he can't come six times in one night!'

*

Mused young Hugh, 'Yes it was last November,
In the organ loft if I remember.
    He took off my cassock,
    Sat me down on a hassock
And made me shake hands with his member.'

*

'And as I shook faster, it grew.
Shot his gism so straight and so true
    That from a distant position,
    He achieved full coition.
Shall I ask him to point it at you?'

*

Years later, that young man called Hugh
Was tossing himself in a pew.
    When reproached by the vicar
    He replied, 'It's far quicker
Than when I took lessons from you!'

This merriment of parsons is mighty offensive.
Letter to Boswell, March 1781
Samuel Johnson 1709-84

There was a young choirgirl from Leek
With periods three times a week.
'Oh dear! Most provoking'
Said the Vicar of Woking.
'Then poking is out — so to speak.'

High up in the Minster at York,
Sat the Organist, Reginald Rourke.
Said the Dean, 'The choir's flat'.
Replied Rourke 'Deaf old bat!
And besides, he's a fine one to talk.'

The prick of old Father McGill
Is tipped with a porcupine quill.
'It looks odd' he'll agree,
'But it does guarantee
To give the most frigid a thrill.'

There was an old girl from East Sheen
Who crept into the vestry, unseen.
    She ripped off her knickers
    And also the Vicar's
And said 'How about it old bean?'

*

Her friend an old spinster of Tottenham
Had no manners, or else she'd forgotten 'em.
    For at tea, at the Vicar's
    She ripped off her knickers.
'Because' she explained, she 'felt 'ot in 'em!'

I have heard with admiring submission the experience
of the lady who declared that the sense of being
well-dressed gives a feeling of inward tranquility which
religion is powerless to bestow.

Letters and Social Aims
Ralph Waldo Emerson 1803-82

The Curate of Dunstan St Just,
Consumed with erotical lust,
    Raped the Vicar's prize fowl,
    Three geese and an owl —
And a poor little budgie, that bust.

Mother Abbess was startled and shocked
To find nuns where the candles were locked.
        Said the Abbess, 'You nuns
        Should behave just like guns,
And never go off 'till you're cocked.'

                    Get thee to a nunnery.
                            Hamlet
            William Shakespeare 1564-1616

There was a young monk of Siberia
Who, of wanking grew wearier and wearier,
        'Til at last, with a yell,
        He burst forth from his cell
And buggered the Father Superior.

An old Buddhist monk from North China
Declared, 'There are few things diviner
        Than to sit in one's cell
        And let one's mind dwell
On the charms of the virgin vagina.'

Three old deaconesses from Kent
Gave up copulation for Lent.
>   This included broom handles,
>   Milk bottles and candles
And anything else, straight or bent!

∞₰∞

The inspiring Cathedral at Rheims
Has featured in many wet dreams.
>   It may look like a phallus,
>   But bear it no malice.
'Twas the builders' intention it seems.

∞₰∞

There once was a pious young priest
Who existed entirely on yeast.
>   Said he 'It is plain
>   We must all rise again.
So I thought I'd get started at least.'

∞₰∞

There was an old strumpet from Cheadle
Who imparted the clap to the Beadle.
>   When she asked 'Does it itch?'
>   He replied, 'Yes, you damned bitch.
And it burns like hell-fire when I peedle!'

Religion is by no means a proper subject of
conversation in mixed company.
Letter to his Godson
Philip Dormer Stanhope,
Earl of Chesterfield 1694-1773

In the jungle, a cleric called Avery
Was captured and sold into slavery.
He escaped with his life,
But alas for his wife,
His sermons are now high-pitched and quavery.

Though devout, Mrs Eileen O'Grady
Has one habit unseemly and shady.
Her farts during service
Make communicants nervous —
Though she eases them out like a lady.

Said an innocent choirboy named Shelley
As the Dean rolled him onto his belly,
'This can't be the position
For proper coition:
And why the petroleum jelly?'

A vicar from near Brentford Dock
Has a uniquely adjustable cock.
　　A remarkable feature
　　Which enables this preacher
To satisfy all of his flock.

Things have come to a pretty pass when religion is
allowed to invade the sphere of private life.
　　　　Remark on hearing an evangelical sermon
　　　　William Lamb, Viscount Melbourne 1779-1848

Have you heard of the Vicar of Kew
Who processed with his cassock askew?
　　An old spinster named Morgan
　　Caught a glimpse of his organ,
And fainted away in her pew!

❧

In Malta, the Dean of Valletta
Met a maiden, and couldn't forget her.
　　So he thought he'd enshrine her
　　As the Holy Vagina
In the Church of the Sacred French Letter.

Have you heard of old Father McGrath
Who screws everything in his path?
    With speed most uncanny
    He ravished the fanny
Of his granny, bent over the bath.

The devotion of Father McMears
To chubby choirboys and their rears
    Must appear to his God
    As perverted and odd.
Perhaps he is one of those queers?

As the French say, there are three sexes — men,
women, and clergymen.
                Rev. Sydney Smith 1771-1845

A devout Christian nudist from Fleet
Loved to dance in the snow and the sleet.
    But one chilly November,
    With a frostbitten member,
He went off, with a friend, on retreat.

There was a young maiden of Harwich
Who was a disgrace at her marriage.
	She proceeded, on skates,
	To the parish church gates,
With the bridesmaids in tow, in a carriage.

An Anglican vicar from Devon
Declared 'I have only had seven
	Nice choirboys to date,
	But I'll soon make it eight,
And shortly thereafter eleven!'

A young cockney girl from up East
In bed was an able artiste;
	For she'd learnt each position
	And the art of coition
In the bed of the old parish priest.

A pretty young curate from Clywd
Would flee from the girls if pursuéd.
	But he was caught one fine day
	And seduced in the hay,
Where he lost all his seminal fluid!

THE BELLS OF HEAVEN

'Twould ring the bells of Heaven
The wildest peal for years,
If Parson lost his senses
And people came to theirs.
The Bells of Heaven
Ralph Hodgson 1871-1962

These verses, one can't but surmise
Were not meant for clerical eyes.
Should any bishop or dean
Find out what they mean,
They ought to blush pink with surprise!

There was a young lady of Chichester,
Whose looks made the saints in their niches stir.
And her full-bodied figure,
Her vim and her vigour
Made the Bishop of Chichester's breeches stir.

An unhappy old Bishop of Fife
Had a nymphomaniacal wife.
    For while he preached to his flock,
        Up the tower — near the clock —
Her keen copulations were rife.

        Brandy for the Parson,
        'Baccy for the Clerk;
            A Smuggler's Song
        Rudyard Kipling 1865-1936

Said the Bishop, 'Now Mary O'Morgan,
Did the vicar uncover his organ?'
    Said the lass, 'I'm not sure.
    I've not seen one before —
But 'twas more like a flute than an organ.'

❧

I'm the Bishop of Brighton and Hove
And a somewhat peculiar cove.
    For I oft take to bed
    Little boys, who are dead —
After warming them up — on a stove!'

The naughty old Bishop of Birmingham
Used to rodger the girls while confirming 'em.
    Midst roars of applause
    He'd rip off their drawers
And pump his episcopal sperm in 'em.

*

And there's more on the Bishop of Birmingham —
What he did to the *boys* while confirming 'em.
    As they knelt on the hassock,
    He'd rip open his cassock,
Then pump his episcopal sperm in 'em.

*

Here's news of more scandal concerning 'im,
That dirty old Bishop of Birmingham.
    He gobbles the choir
    As they sing 'Ave Maria'
And fondles them all if confirming 'em.

*

But the choir reaped revenge up in Birmingham
On the Bishop as he was confirming 'em.
    While they knelt in their stalls,
    They tickled his balls.
Now please no more stories concerning 'em!

———'s idea of Heaven is eating *pâtés de foie gras* to the sound of trumpets.

                                        Rev. Sydney Smith 1771-1845

The Bishop of Worcester, how rude,
Loved to romp with this blonde, in the nude.
  But she moaned 'Oh my Lord;
  With plain screwing I'm bored.
Can't we try to do something that's lewd?'

A cardinal, living in Rome,
Installed a Greek bath in his home,
  Full of statues, undraped
  With bums nicely shaped.
He loved to toss-off in the foam.

The Bishop of Durham would preach
Above love, which he wanted to teach.
  But his sex life was ended
  By a paunch so distended,
It annulled, *ipso facto*, his reach.

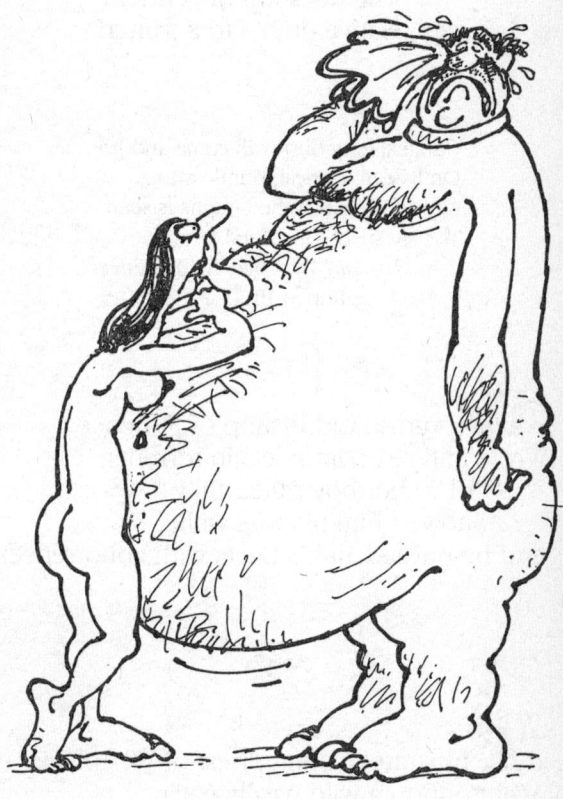

The Anglican Bishop of Ceuta
Enjoys sex with a lad, lass or neuter.
      For as long as they're tender
      The question of gender
Is a relative one — to a fruiter!

Curates, long dust, will come and go
On lissom, clerical, printless toe;
And oft between the boughs is seen
The sly shade of a Rural Dean.
        The Old Vicarage, Granchester
              Rupert Brooke 1887-1915

The prudish old Bishop of Florence
Wrote anti-sex pamphlets in torrents;
      'Til a choirboy called Billy
      Showed him his wee willie,
And he burned all his tracts with abhorrence.

A frustrated young priest of Westphalia
Went out on a wild bacchanalia.
      He rogered a nun —
      Screwed a friar for fun,
Then the Bishop, in fullest regalia.

Asked what he desired most of all,
'A penis' said the Pope named John Paul.
    Coughed a cardinal 'No.
    It is not pronounced so.
But 'appiness, if I recall.'

OVER THE HILLS AND FAR AWAY

Tom, the Piper's Son c. 1795

A travelling salesman called Wright
Could travel much faster than light.
    He set off one day
    In a relative way,
And came back the previous night!

Oh, to be in England, now that April's there.
Home-thoughts, from Abroad
Robert Browning 1812-89

In Perth lived a virile young punk
With a tool like an elephant's trunk.
    When this prick pachydermatous
    Shot a hot stream of sperm at us,
We were showered, head to foot, in his spunk.

Through back alleys near Wuthering Heights
I creep around, peeping at nights.
　　Through most keyholes I peep
　　I spy folk fast asleep,
But I do see some marvellous sights!

❧

A yokel who lived in Devizes
Had bollocks of differing sizes.
　　One, weighing a pound,
　　Dragged along on the ground.
The other was small as a fly's is.

*

We've all heard of the man from Devizes,
The winner of numerous prizes;
　　His prick, when at ease,
　　Hangs down to his knees,
And tickles his chin when it rises.

❧

A worried teenager from Poole
Discovered red rings on his tool.
　　Said the doctor — a cynic —
　　'Get out of my clinic!
Just wipe off the lipstick — damned fool!'

On the stage at a rally in Kew,
Wearing Union Jack drawers of bright hue,
     Margaret — dashed bad form —
     Spread her knees — it was warm.
Heckler, 'Down with the red, white and blue!'

In a dream, an old Brummie from Greet
Was screwed, in the nude, in New Street.
     But the best of the joke
     Was when she awoke
And found mud on her bum and her feet.

Stands the Church Clock at ten to three?
And is there honey still for tea?

Sorry dear — Honey's off.
          The Old Vicarage, Granchester
Rupert Brooke 1887-1915 (with additional
          acknowledgements to Peter Sellers)

They bake funny buns in Nuneaton
With dough that's first whipped and then beaten.
     They consume several tons
     Of these fabulous buns,
But outside the town there's none eaten.

There was an eccentric old boffin
Who remarked, in a fierce fit of coughin',
    'It isn't the cough
    That carries you off.
But the coffin they carry you off in.'

❦

There was an old spinster from Wemyss
Who, it seems, was afflicted by dreams.
    She'd awake in the night
    In a terrible fright
And rattle the rooftops with screams.

❦

An anaemic old spinster from Stoke,
Who in favour of chastity spoke,
    By her GP was told
    'If I may make so bold,
What you need is a jolly good poke!'

❦

There was a drunk lady of Twickenham
Whose shoes were too tight to move quick in 'em.
    She went out for a run,
    Which she shouldn't have done —
Then took 'em both off and was sick in 'em!

Fred Longbottom, climbing Ben Nevis,
Fell fifty feet into a crevice.
 Wedged there by *Ars Longa*
 He recovered — grew stronger,
Then pegged out. Poor Fred. *Vita Brevis!*

 In summertime on Bredon
 The bells they sound so clear;
 Bredon Hill
 Alfred Edward Housman 1859-1936

An MP, while dining at Crewe,
Once found a dead mouse in his stew.
 Said the waiter 'Don't shout
 And wave it about.
Or the rest will be wanting one too.'

Last winter a woman from Surrey,
Who needed to pee in a hurry,
 Dashed straight round the back
 And opened her crack
Thus causing a sleet and snow flurry.

In Bradford, a stupid young nutter
Was trying to write 'cunt' on a shutter.
    He had got to 'C-U-'
    When a pious Hindu
Kicked him arse over tit in the gutter.

A brickie from over the water
Day by day became shorter and shorter.
    The reason, he said
    Was the hod on his head,
Which was filled with the heaviest mortar.

His sister, who lived down in Pinner,
Grew constantly thinner and thinner.
    The reason was plain:
    She slept out in the rain,
And was never allowed any dinner.

With acknowledgements to Lewis Carrol.

Near Evesham, a man from the Vale
Was out, one fine day, shooting quail,
    When he tripped on a rock
    And so damaged his cock
That now he is not very male.

A manic depressive from Troon
Had a longing to die very soon.
    For he hadn't the luck
    To've been got by a fuck
But by a toss-off, shoved in with a spoon.

∞⚘∞

There was an old woman of Ryde
Who ate some sour apples and died.
    The apples fermented
    Inside the lamented,
Making cider inside her inside.

*

Then, sadly, her sister from Ryde
Fell into a sewer and died.
    The next day their brother
    Fell into another.
So now they're interred side by side.

∞⚘∞

A young man on the train home from Stoke
Unbuttoned his flies for a joke.
    Two girls gave a shout,
    An old spinster passed out,
And an elderly queer had a stroke!

God; I will pack, and take a train,
And get me to England once again;
The Old Vicarage, Granchester
Rupert Brooke 1887-1915

There was a young man from Thames Ditton,
Who thought Sartre and Freud unbefittin',
    While Marcuse and McLuhan
    He felt were just doin'
What's commonly known as bull-shittin'.

❧

For a dare, a young gardener from Leeds
Once swallowed a packet of seeds.
    In a month his smooth arse
    Was all covered in grass
And his bollocks grown over with weeds.

Our England is a garden that is full of stately views ...
The Glory of the Garden
Rudyard Kipling 1865-1936

LANDS BEYOND THE SEA

I travelled among unknown men
In lands beyond the sea;
Nor, England! did I know til then
What love I bore to thee.
I Travelled among Unknown Men
William Wordsworth 1770-1850

An old peasant woman near Umsk
Was wholly unable to cumsk.
But there was an ecstatic shout
When a samovar spout
Was shoved up her Muscovite rumpsk!

An ugly old rat-bag from France,
At whom every man looked askance,
Put a sack on her head
And then jumped into bed,
Saying 'At least I've now got half a chance!'

A nosey milkman of Calcutta
Saw his wife through a chink in a shutter.
    He could hear her deep sighs
    And see the firm thighs
And the bum of the boy who was up 'er.

*

With frustration, the milkman did mutter
And began to toss off in the gutter.
    But the hot searing sun
    Put paid to his fun,
'Cos it curdled his cream into butter.

Goodbye Piccadilly, Farewell Leicester Square.
                    Alice Smith B. Jay fl.1908

There was a young geisha from China
Who mixed up her mouth and vagina.
    Her clitoris huge
    She smothered with rouge,
And lipsticked her labia minor.

There was an old man of Tashkent,
Whose tool was irreparably bent.
    So, to save himself trouble
    He put it in double.
But instead of coming — he went!

There was a plump girl from Australia
Who went to a dance as a dahlia.
    Alas — the petals uncurled
    And declared to the world
Both the dress and its contents a failure.

Greek passions are carefree and furious
And their excesses sometimes most injurious.
    And though famed for great zest,
    On the Sabbath they rest
In a manner Melina Mercourious.

There was an old man of Madras
Whose balls were made of brass.
    In windy weather
    They clanged together
And sparks flew out of his arse.

A mandarin's wife from Shanghai
Was more than exceedingly shy:
    For when undressing at night,
    She'd turn out the light,
For fear of the all-seeing eye!

An' there ain' no 'buses runnin' from the Bank to
Mandalay.

Mandalay
Rudyard Kipling 1865-1936

An old Chinese poet named Woo
Fell asleep in a rubber canoe.
    He was dreaming that coolies
    Were tickling his goolies,
When he woke up all covered in glue!

Hells Angels en route through Pretoria
Gang-banged a young virgin named Gloria.
    That was two weeks ago
    And as far as we know
She is still in a state of euphoria!

A tourist named Thomas from Truro
On a Portuguese package in Douro
    Tried to 'make' sweet Conchita,
    But the chaste señorita
Keeps her naughty bits locked in a bureau.

❦

A hot-tempered girl of Carracas
Had a husband, a two timing jackas.
    When he started to cheat her
    With a dark señorita,
She kicked him hard — in the marracas!

❦

An old Irish lady called Lil
Used a dynamite stick for a thrill.
    They found her vagina
    In South Carolina
And bits of her tits in Brazil!

Go west, young man.
John Babsone Lane Soule 1815-91

An arrogant madam from Djerba
Declared that no prick could peturb 'er,
    'Til a Price of Arabia
    Knocked the hell from her labia
With his fifteen-inch fanny disturber!

Ship me somewheres east of Suez, where the best is
like the worst,
Where there aren't no Ten Commandments, an' a man
can raise a thirst:

Mandalay
Rudyard Kipling 1865-1936

Mrs Marcos, ex-Queen of Manilla,
Whose panties were lined with Chinchilla,
    Said 'Two things great wealth brings —
    A taste for fine things
And plenty of shoes in my villa.'

BOYS AND GIRLS

Boys and girls come out to play,
The moon doth shine as bright as day.
Useful Transactions in Philosophy
William King fl. 1708

It's time to make love, douse the glim.
The fireflies twinkle and dim.
    The stars gleam together
    Like birds of a feather
And the loin lies down with the limb.

Conrad Aiken, b 1889

There was a fair lady called Starkey
Who had an affair with a darkie.
    The results of her sins
    Were quadruplets — not twins;
One black, one white and two khaki.

There was a young fellow of Beaulieu
Who loved a fair maiden most truly.
    Begged he 'Please be mine!'
    And as she didn't decline,
The marriage was solemnised duly.

Mox nox in rem.
Let's get on with it!

A frustrated virgin named Soame
Told her boyfriend one midnight in Rome:
    'If that willie stays dead
    You can hop out of bed,
Get dressed and then piss off back home!'

An inquisitive virgin called Dora
Asked her boyfriend, who'd started to bore 'er,
    'Do you mean birds and bees
    Go through antics like these
To provide us with fauna and flora?'

There was a young fellow called Jed
Whose organ was big and blood-red.
    Said his girlfriend, 'Your prick
    Is too long and too thick.
Let's go to the pictures instead.'

Amantes sunt amentes.
Lovers are lunatics.

There was a young lady called Sue
Who preferred a stiff drink to a screw.
    But the one leads to the other
    And now she's a mother.
Let that be a lesson to you.

HAPPY FAMILIES

All happy families resemble each other; each unhappy
family is unhappy in its own way.

Anna Karenina
Leo Tolstoy 1828-1910

A spotty young schoolboy named Ned
Used to masturbate nightly in bed.
    Said his mother, 'Dear lad,
    That's exceedingly bad.
Jump in with your mama instead.'

There's a bounder who lived in Cape Cod
Who put his own mother in pod.
    His name? It was Tucker.
    The dirty young fucker.
The bastard! The bugger! The sod!

An ambitious old fellow named Plumb
Had a son who was stupid and dumb.
    When he urged him ahead
    He went down instead;
For he thought to succeed meant succumb!

Accidents will occur in the best-regulated families.
Mr Micawber in *David Copperfield*
Charles Dickens 1812-70

A tetchy young woman from Itchen
Was scratching her snatch in the kitchen:
    When her mother said, 'Rose.
    It's the pox I suppose?'
Replied 'Bollocks! Get on with your stitchin'.'

There was a young welder from Reading
Who was constantly wetting the bedding,
    'Till his mother one day,
    In a wearisome way,
Suggested a girl and a wedding!

A forward young fellow named Carr
Had a longing for sex — with his Ma.
    'Go and play with your sister'
    Said she, when he kissed her.
'I've problems enough with your Pa!'

*Dos linages sólos hay en el mundo, como decía una
abuela mía, que son el tenir y el no tenir.*
There are but two families in the world, as my
grandmother used to say; the Haves and the Have-nots.
                              Don Quixote
                Miguel de Cervantes 1547-1616

When Oedipus plunged in — erect,
Jocasta cried 'Cease. I object.
    You're a Greek. Screw some other
    Like your friend or your brother.
Mother-fucking is somewhat suspect.'

                Birds in their little nests agree
                And 'tis a shameful sight,
                When members of one family
                Fall out, and chide, and fight.
Divine Songs for Children, xvi Against Quarrelling
                    Isaac Watts 1674-1748

A young man with passions most gingery,
Tore a hole in his sister's best lingerie.
    And having goosed her behind
    He made up his mind
To add incest to insult and injury.

STRUMPETS AND THEIR ILK

The silver, snarling (s)trumpets 'gan to chide.
The Eve of St Agnes.
John Keats 1795-1821

An elderly gent in Baroda
Refused an old pro what he owed her.
Said she, 'What a prick.
Expects screwing on tick!'
So she pissed in his whisky and soda.

One glance at the whores of Bombay
Turns any man ashen and grey.
They've got thin sagging breasts
On their boney old chests,
And they carry their bums on a tray!

Said a strumpet from Newton-le-Willows
While placing two polka-dot pillows
    Beneath her trim bum,
    'Sex is sinful to some.
But to me men are mere peckerdillos!'

An insatiable strumpet named Annie
Had fleas, lice and crabs in her fanny.
    Getting into her flue
    Was like a trip to the zoo.
Wild beasts lurked in each nook and cranny.

There was a young man from Belgrade
Who slept with a whore in the trade.
    Said she 'Look here Jack.
    Try the hole round the back,
As the front one is badly decayed!'

Van Gogh found a whore he could lay
Who'd accept a small painting as pay.
    'Long liff aart!' cried Van Gogh.
    'But 'tis neffer enoff.
I vish I could paint ten a day!'

There was an old pro of Kilkenny
Whose fee for a screw was a penny.
    But for half of that sum
    Her round rosy bum
Was a source of amusement to many.

Ubi mel ibi apes.
Where there's honey there's bees.

A brazen old whore from Zambezi
Said 'Attracting the men is quite easy.
    And this is because
    I never wear drawers
And stand somewhere that's frightfully breezy.'

A greedy seed merchant from Goring
Insisted his wife should go whoring.
    And — I can put it in writing —
    Though *he* found it exciting,
She found it exceedingly boring.

A harlot from Mornington Crescent
Always failed to make men acquiescent
    To her lewd proposition:
    For they knew that coition
Wasn't safe with a cunt so putrescent.

During screwing, a strumpet from Woking
Reacted so much to the poking
    That her gyratory motion
    Caused such heat and commotion
That her pussy and pubes started smoking.

The harlots who come from Devizes
Can accommodate cocks of all sizes,
    From one inch to ten —
    Which covers most men.
Those longer then ten receive prizes.

SCHOOLDAYS: THE HAPPIEST DAYS OF ONE'S LIFE

I only took the regular course … the different branches of Arithmetic — Ambition, Distraction, Uglification and Derision.

Alice in Wonderland.
Lewis Carroll (Charles Lutwidge Dodgson) 1832-98

A stubborn King's Scholar at Eton,
Whose backside had often been beaten,
    Was either prepared,
    So the Provost declared,
Or else had been secretly cheatin'.

There was a young scholar at Harrow
Who moaned that his mouth was too narrow.
    For times without number
    He'd eat a cucumber,
But never could manage a marrow.

Let schoolmasters puzzle their brain,
With grammar, and nonsense, and learning.
Good liquor, I stoutly maintain,
Gives genius a better discerning.

She Stoops to Conquer
Oliver Goldsmith 1728-74

While old Chalky writes up a declension,
We schoolboys do things one can't mention:
    Like tossing and blowing
    Each other, and showing
A singular lack of attention.

❧

A thrify young schoolgirl from Shoreham
Made some brown paper knickers and wore 'em.
    They looked nice and neat
    'Til she bent down in the street
To pick up a pin — and she tore 'em.

❧

A despairing schoolmistress named Beauchamp
Wailed 'Boys! I just cannot teach 'em.
    I try to look grave
    But they will not behave,
Though with tears in my eyes I beseech 'em.'

'Now look here Montgomery Major, if you don't make
this bed properly, you and I are going to fall out!'
                                    Preparatory School Matron

A young public school man named Teddy
With the juniors used to go steady
    'Til the nosey old Head
    Caught the bounder in bed
With a fourth-former — upturned and ready.

A young Wykehamist enquired 'Who
Will show me the way to the loo?
    For I must have a piss
    And in addition to this,
I'm just itchin' to masturbate too.'

When Jane and young Marcus first fiddled
At school, she cried out 'I've been diddled!'
    For she found he'd a cock
    While she, 'neath her frock,
Had only the hole where she tiddled!

A young convent schoolgirl named Randle
Used to frig herself off with a candle.
    One day in the gym
    It shot forth from her quim,
Which started a very grave scandal.

Aut disce aut discede.
Either learn or leave.

When Sue stripped in the Easter Parade
Such a stunning impression she made
    That the boys of St Paul's
    To a man burst their balls,
And had to be given first aid.

A kinky old chaplain at Eton
Adored, with the birch, to be beaten.
    He loved to bend low
    With his buttocks aglow,
And 'twas cheaper than turning the heat on.

A lively young schoolgirl from Cheltenham
Put tights on to see how she felt in 'em.
    But she soon gave a shout —
    'Oh Lawks — get me out.
I've a fear that my fanny will melt in 'em!'

Our teacher drank so much strong tea
That when she went out for a pee
    And pulled on the chain
    She was flushed down the drain.
And by now she's ten miles out to sea.

No Better Than She Should Be!

Varium et mutabile semper femina.
Woman is ever fickle and changeable. You are no
better than you should be.

The Coxcomb
John Fletcher 1579-1625

A naked young temptress called Titty
Lies nude on the beach — very pretty.
    'Hey. No, Stop,' she blurts.
    'Pull it out quick. It hurts.
You've been in the sand and it's gritty!'

An insatiable woman from Chester
Declared as an old man undressed her:
    'I'll only regret
    The fact that we met
If the lips of my fanny should fester.'

A sweet disorder in the dress
Kindles in clothes a wantonness:
Hesperides. Delight in Disorder
Robert Herrick 1591-1674

Whilst practicing sexual contortions
It's wise to take proper precautions.
    Poor Ermintrude
    Let a sperm intrude.
Does anyone here do abortions?

Our topless barlady, Lil West,
Serves cocktails direct from the breast.
    Her right tit gives cherry,
    The left one strawberry,
And there's Pernod, by special request.

Moaned a luscious young lady named Wade
On the beach, with her charms all displayed,
    'It's so hot in the sun:
    Perhaps sex would be fun.
At least it would give me some shade.'

The passionate pussy of Fran
Exhausts the most virile young man.
　　But occasionally — maybe —
　　This results in a baby.
But she flushes them all down the pan.

⚓

There was a young lady of Pinner
Whose hubby came home for his dinner.
　　And the first thing he saw
　　When he opened the door
Was the bum of the bloke who was in 'er.

*

The bloke who got caught was called Tupper.
He fled home to his wife for his supper.
　　And guess what *he* saw
　　When he opened *his* door?
The balls of the bloke who was up 'er!!

Madam, a circulating library in a town is as an
evergreen tree of diabolical knowledge! It blossoms
throughout the year! And depend on it, Mrs Malaprop,
that they who are so fond of handling the leaves will
long for the fruit at last.

The Rivals
Richard Brinsley Sheridan 1751-1816

Have you heard of Miss Foo Foo La Rue,
Who thinks it's great fun just to screw?
  She is never particular
  But prefers perpendicular —
An art known to only a few.

Shirley's face is all careworn and ashen;
The result of insatiable passion.
  Although she knows it's not right,
  She screws hard, day and night,
Just in case it should go out of fashion.

  Change in a trice
  The lilies and languors of virtue
  For the raptures and roses of vice.
Atalanta in Calydon. Collected Poetical Works (1924)
    Algernon Charles Swinburne 1837-1909

There once were three trollops of Twickenham
Who loved to have plenty of prick in 'em.
  They knelt and implored
  And petitioned the Lord
To lengthen and strengthen and thicken 'em.

  Miss Buss and Miss Beale
  Cupid's darts do not feel.
  How different from us,
  Miss Beale and Miss Buss.
Of the Headmistress of the North London Collegiate
 School and the Principal of the Ladies' College,
   Cheltenham (Anon, 19th century).

FABLES OF FUR,
FEATHER AND FLEECE

When raped by four apes in Rangoon,
A torrid young tourist named June
    Said 'I adored the wild screwing
    Those gorillas were doing:
But why did they all come so soon!'

This field, by old Farmer McGraw,
Is held in great reverence and awe.
    For here, on this spot
    He had his first piece of twat,
While her mother stood by and said 'Baa'!

    Baa, baa, black sheep,
    Have you any wool?
    Yes sir, yes sir,
    Three bags full:
    One for the master,
    And one for the dame,
    And one for the little boy
    Who lives down the lane.

Tommy Thumb's Pretty Song Book (c. 1744)

A lusty farm lad, for a joke,
Gave the hens in the farmyard a poke.
But his vice was betrayed
When the eggs that they laid
Held nothing but white with no yolk.

There was a young maiden named Muffet,
Who sat on a dildo-shaped tuffet.
There came a fat spider
Which offered to ride her:
But she scoffed at the size of its stuffet!

There was a young man from Geneva
Who buggered a black bitch retriever.
The result was a sow,
Two llamas, a cow,
Three horses, a duck and a beaver.

There was an old fellow from Nice
Who tried to make love to two geese.
But he went just too far
With the budgerigar
And his parrot rang up the police.

Eiusdem farinae.
Birds of a Feather.

One Christmas a spinster named Thrasher,
After three drinks grew bolder and brasher.
First she screwed Santa Claus,
Then without any pause
Had Donner and Blitzen and Dasher.

✿

A wonderful bird is the pelican;
His bill will hold more than his belly can.
He can take, in his beak
Food enough for a week.
But I'm damned if I know how the hell he can!

✿

A young matador from Madrid
Quite fancied a screw with a squid.
But as he plunged his stiff rod
In the cephalopod,
It squirted its ink — Yes it did!

✿

There once was an orangoutingue
Who would eat nothing else but meringue.
As he sat on the floor,
Having gorged forty-four,
That stupid old monkey went bingue!

There was a short-kilted North Briton,
Who, for kinkiness, sat on a kitten.
    But the pussy had claws;
    The immediate cause
Of his somewhat abrupt circumcision.

'The harlots of London are frightful;
And the fairies? My dear, they're so spiteful.
    But I'm no longer on heat
    For I happened to meet
A sheep in Hyde Park — quite delightful.'

The farmhand climbed onto a stool
To ram his long prick up a mule.
    But just as he'd started,
    The animal farted
And blew H_2S up his tool.

There was a strange fellow from Dover
Who yearned for a romp in the clover.
    But he gave not one damn
    For a woman or man.
The clue was his cry of 'Here Rover'!

FAIRIES AT THE BOTTOM
OF THE GARDEN

There are fairies at the bottom of our garden.
Fairies and Chimneys
Rose Fyleman 1877-1957

A merchant from far-off Kashmir
Is known to be frightfully queer.
    For his major sex joys
    Are with fat bottomed boys.
He's not seen his wife this past year!

'Seven Pillars of Wisdom' they say
Is a volume reputedly gay.
    To put it quite plain,
    T.E. Lawrence liked pain,
And preferred things the masochists' way.

Have you heard 'bout the Bailiff of Neath
Who screws pixies who live on the Heath?
    His runcible dong
    Is so terribly long
It emerges between their front teeth!

An effete aesthete, Frilly Fred
To a fruity young friend sadly said,
    'When I woke up last night
    Can you imagine my fright
To find a nude girl in my bed?'

There was a scout-master named Duckham
Who loved little boys and would suck 'em.
    And when their willies grew longer
    And their buttocks were stonger
He'd whip off his Y-fronts and fuck 'em.

    Oh 'tis a glorious thing, I ween,
    To be a regular Royal Queen!
    No half-and-half affair, I mean,
    But a right-down regular Royal Queen!
                 The Gondoliers
    Sir William Schwenk Gilbert 1836-1911

The Head of the Nazi SA
Was commonly thought to be gay.
    He'd caper through Munich
    In sandals and tunic
Singing 'I'm the Queen of the May.'

There was a young actor named Mallory
Who gobbled his boss in the gallery.
    He agreed, with some wit,
    'Yes, I may be a shit,
But look at the size of my salary.'

Says he, 'I am a handsome man, but I'm a gay deceiver.'
Love Laughs at Locksmiths
George Colman 1726-1836

A pretty young man from Southend
Decried sodomy to a friend.
    Chimed in an old queer,
    'Don't worry my dear,
You'll find it's quite nice — in the end!'

Said a shrewd businessman from Belgrade,
Whose mind dwelled on commerce and trade,
      'I will suck without charge
      Any cock, if it's large.
If it's not, I expect to be paid.'

The callers on kinky Miss Fay
Her neighbours believe are all gay.
      For none, when they call
      Use her front door at all.
They always go in the back way!

Two dykes went their separate routes.
Affirmed one, 'I don't give two hoots.
      For no interest linked us
      Except cunilingus
And a penchant for dark pin-striped suits!'

'Curiouser and curiouser!' cried Alice.
Alice's Adventures in Wonderland
Lewis Carroll (Charles Lutwidge Dodgson) 1832-98

There was an old roué from Rome
Who took a young leprechaun home.
  As he was buggering the elf
  He thought to himself,
'I'd be much better off in a gnome.'

A fair-haired young fellow from Fleet,
Who minced as he walked down the street,
  Wore shoes of bright red
  And suggestively said,
'I may not be strong, but I'm sweet.'

A dirty old man of Madrid
Cast lewd eyes on a plump-bottomed kid.
  Quoth he 'Oh what joy!
  I'll bugger that boy.
You see if I don't.' — and he did!

The only way to get rid of a temptation is to yield to it.
The Picture of Dorian Grey
Oscar Wilde 1854-1900

There are some things men mustn't expose;
So they hide them away in their clothes.
  And it's thought rude to stare
  At what's bulging there.
But why this is so — Heavens knows.

HE MARCHED THEM UP
TO THE TOP OF THE HILL

The noble Duke of York,
He had ten thousand men,
He marched them up to the top of the hill,
And he marched them down again.
And when they were up, they were up,
And when they were down, they were down,
And when they were only half way up,
They were neither up nor down.

First printed in *Mother Goose*
Arthur Rackham (1913)

The colonel cried out with great force
In the midst of Hyde Park for a horse.
   All his soldiers searched round
   But none could be found.
So he just rhododendron, of course!

And though hard be the task,
'Keep a stiff upper-lip'.
Keep a Stiff Upper Lip
Phoebe Cary 1824-71

A Scots Guardsman, who came from Glasgow,
Was asked what he wore down below.
    With a tilt of the kilt
    He replied 'If tha wilt
Tha may'st feel for thaself — then tha'll'st know!'

A frustrated young Royal Marine
Has invented a screwing machine.
    Concave and convex,
    It will fit either sex,
And is ever so simple to clean.

In utrumque paratus.
Ready come what may.

A REME man, based up in Alnwick
Had leanings most anti-Germanic.
    So when war had begun.
    He constructed a gun
With dimensions quite simply titanic.

The Hussars' own choleric colonel
Used language obscene and infernal.
    The poor Padre, aghast,
    Gave up protest at last.
And wrote it all down in his journal.

༄

Said a young Irish Guardsman from Buckingham
'As for girls, I do quite fancy fucking 'em.
    But when I meet boys —
    Wow! How I enjoys
Just licking their dickies and sucking 'em.'

War is much too serious a thing to be left to military
men.
            Quoted by Briand to Lloyd George during
                    the Great War, 1914-1918
            Charles-Maurice de Talleyrand 1754-1838

An argie flew to the Malvinas
In one of those old Catalinas.
    He pulled back on the stick
    With an action so quick
That he fractured his co-pilot's penis.

The General's wife, in Bengal,
As a newspaper went to a ball.
  But the journal caught fire
  And burnt her entire
Front page, sporting section and all.

A colonel (retired) deep in Surrey
Demanded 'A dashed good goat curry.'
  But what was served on the tray
  From the new 'Take-Away'
Had a taste more like goat poop or slurry!

A nymphomaniacal WAAC
Possessed a libidinous knack.
  Her erotic resources
  So pleased the armed forces
That she spent the whole war on her back.

THE HORN OF THE HUNTER

The horn of the hunter is heard on the hill:
                    Kathleen Mavourneen
                    Metropolitan Magazine, London
                    Julia Crawford fl.1835

Miss Muffett slumped back in the corn;
Her clothes were all tattered and torn.
        For it wasn't the spider
        That had sat down beside her.
'Twas Little Boy Blue, with his horn!

An expatriate Scotsman in Durham
Makes the girls in those parts squeal and squr-um.
        He withdraws, then lets fly,
        Shouting 'Mud in your eye!'
Which is where he deposits his sper-um!

What he asked for – a four-letter word
Badly frightened the frigid Miss Bird.
>   But large gins and insistence
>   Wore away her resistance,
And that four-letter word then occurred!

There was a young fellow called Menzies
Whose kissing sent girls into frenzies.
>   But a shy virgin one night
>   Crossed her legs in a fright
And fractured his bi-focal lenses!

This insatiable fellow named Blades –
His favourite fruit was young maids;
>   But sheep, boys and whores
>   And the knot holes in doors
Were by no means exempt from his raids.

A once buxom typist called Valerie
On a diet did count every calorie.
>   Said her boss, in disgust,
>   'You've lost half your bust!
So you're only worth half of your salary.'

AND THE TRUMPET SHALL SOUND

You must stir it and stump it,
And blow your own trumpet,
Or trust me, you haven't a chance.
Ruddigore
Sir William Schwenck Gilbert 1836-1911

An elderly lady of Brent
Always farted wherever she went.
One day at the fair
She dropped a few there,
So they plugged up her bum with cement.

A flatulent cockney called Billy
Could fart like a two-year old filly.
He did it so well
That he once blew to hell
The lavatories 'neath Piccadilly.

In the Tate an art student named Roma
Laid a fart with such foetid aroma
    That her sphincter corroded
    And her knickers exploded –
Which won her a Fine Art Diploma.

The rumblynge of a fart, and every soun,
Nis but of eir reverberacioun ...

The rumbling of a fart or any sound
Is only air reverberating round ...
          The Summoner's Tale
       Geoffrey Chaucer c.1340-1400
       (translated by Nevill Coghill)

In Iceland, a wonderful wizzard
Had discomfort deep down in his gizzard.
    So he gulped wind and snow –
    It was fifty below –
Then farted a forty day blizzard.

There was an old girl of La Plata
Who was widely acclaimed as a farter.
    At the Argentine sports
    Her defeaning reports
Ensured her much fame as the starter.

There was a young man of Rangoon
Whose farts could be heard on the moon.
　　When least you'd expect 'em
　　They'd erupt from his rectum
With the strength of a raging typhoon.

❧

There was a young milkmaid from Ossett
Who went to the penny-slot closet.
　　But when she got there
　　She could only pass air.
That wasn't a penny's worth – was it?

❧

A flatulent plumber, Fred Hart
Could not get his blow-lamp to start.
　　So he lit up a match
　　Saying 'Now it'll catch.'
'Twas the end of Fred Hart, lamp and fart!

❧

There was a fat fellow from Stroud
Who could fart unbelievably loud.
　　When he let go a big 'un,
　　Dogs were deafened in Wigan
And window panes cracked at St Cloud.

This Nicholas anon leet fle a fart,
As greet as it had been a thonder-dent
That with the strook he was almost yblent.

Then Nicholas at once let fly a fart
As loud as if it were a thunder-clap.
He was near blinded by the blast, poor chap.
                              The Miller's Tale
                    Geoffrey Chaucer c.1340-1400
                    (translated by Nevill Coghill)

There was a old Bey of Calcutta
Who greased up his arsehole with butter.
          And instead of the roar
          Which had come there before,
Came forth a soft oleaginous mutter.

It takes little strain and no art
To let rip an echoing fart.
          I enjoy rectal violence
          In moments of siolence,
And snigger when bystanders start.

*

It takes little skill and no art
To let out a foul-smelling fart.
          If you fart at a party
          Some reaction is hearty
But the sensitive persons depart.

AS A STUDENT OF THE HUMAN CONDITION AND, TO MY everlasting amazement, now a published 'name', I find myself increasingly prevailed upon by my burgeoning congregation to prepare a further collection of limericks.

Convinced as I am of freshly emerging veins of invention and wit beyond my somewhat parochial ambit, I feel it is my duty to extend to the reader, and any attendant coterie or salon, an invitation to submit to me any gems of this most virtuous form of literature with which he, or in this modern age, she, may be aquainted.

If outstanding exemplars of the genre were to be addressed to the publishers of this volume, a grateful former Chaplain of St Swithun's would rejoice at such an opportunity to lay before a new generation of scholars and readers a new flowering of the supremely simple five-line verse.

The Reverend Septimus Bunbury
c/o Queen Anne Press
Macdonald & Co (Publishers) Ltd
3rd Floor
Greater London House
Hampstead Road
London NW1 7QX